Pierre Bergé

Yves Saint Laurent
A Moroccan Passion

Drawings by Lawrence Mynott
Translation by José Abete

Abrams, New York

This book was first published in French, with the title "Yves Saint Laurent Une passion marocaine", in connection with the exhibition "Yves Saint Laurent et le Maroc" held at the Jardin Majorelle Museum in Marrakech in November 2010, and at the Villa des Arts in Casablanca in the spring of 2011.

ysl

A wall painting by Yves Saint Laurent (page 62)

In memoriam

Boul de Breteuil

Maurice Doan

Talitha Getty

Joe McPhillips

Robert Parvillée

Fernando Sanchez

Adolfo de Velasco

Bill Willis

It was aboard an Air France Caravelle
jetliner, after a layover in Tangier,
that Yves and I arrived in Marrakech
in February, 1966. We of course
stayed at La Mamounia, which at the
time was a hotel that evoked an
old-world charm. Welcomed by the concierge,
Camille, we discovered a mythical
place that unfortunately would lose
its soul over the years. In 1966,
the past was still alive and well at
La Mamounia. Its rooms and bathrooms
were simple and comfortable, and were
not meant to impress. It was pure luxury.

It was overcast that day, colors everywhere seemed faded, and soon the rain began to fall. It didn't stop raining for an entire week. We would later become familiar with Morocco's rain. That week, as did all other hotel guests, we nervously asked the concierge about the weather. He assured us that so much rain was rare, and that the weather would improve the following day. Since then we have learned to love and even desire rain, and to appreciate its benefits.

One morning we awoke and the sun had appeared. A Moroccan sun that probes every recess and corner. The birds were singing, the snow-capped Atlas Mountains blocked the horizon, and the perfume of jasmine rose to our room. We would never forget that morning, since in a certain way, it decided our destiny.

Suddenly we loved this city, the people, and the country.

This is how Dar el Hanch (The Snake's House)
appeared when Maurice Doan sold it to us.

We so fell in love with everything, that at the end of our trip, while on the flight home, we had in our hands a signed provisional sales agreement to buy a house in the medina- Dar el Hanch - The Snake's House. Our passion for Morocco began that day.

The patio at Dar el Hanch

Yves at Dar el Hanch

Fatima and Majouba, who ran
our house

Yves and Hazel,
our second
Chihuahua

Yves would often go to
the Djemaa el Fna Square

We shared our lives over many years with Mustapha, Boujemaa, Bernard, and Albert. We owe them so much. Each one had what Flaubert called "a simple heart."

Albert arranging flowers

Boujemaa and Hazel

Bernard and Yves

Mustapha

Dar el Hanch was a small house which
we decorated modestly with tables and
chairs found in the souks. The house
bordered a vacant parcel of land which
was called the "lemon garden", behind
which an alleyway led to the Bab Doukkala
mosque.
We spent many happy moments in this
house.

Yves very quickly found a source of
inspiration in Morocco and
Orientalism.

In 1966, Paul and Talitha Getty also
settled in Marrakech. They were just
married, and we quickly became friends.
They bought a palace that would later
belong to Alain Delon and Bernard-Henri
Lévy, who still lives there. The Gettys
arrived with an American decorator,
Bill Willis. We spent many unforgettable
evenings at their palace with Isa
Belline and the painter, Brion Gysin-
inventor of the Dream Machine.

Morocco owes much to Bill Willis, who would play an important role alongside us.

me, Talitha, and Yves. A beautifully tender relationship and friendship

A close friend, Maurice Hogenboom, Talitha, and Hazel Number 2.

The youth, beauty and intelligence of
Yves is so well captured in this photo
by Patrick Lichfield . It represents
for me the perfect reflection and reminder
of our life at Dar el Hanch.

Yves at the Menara gardens

Me at the Menara gardens

Many others, including some who would become friends, arrived in Marrakech at the same time as us. Paul and Talitha Getty seduced us with their extravagance and elegance; Jacqueline Foissac settled in Morocco and would become a renowned decorator. She arrived with her son, Quito; he was then still a child and would later become so close to Yves and me. Adolfo de Velasco, who would organise dinners and lunches to which everyone wanted to be invited; Arndt and Hetti von Bohlen who we immediately loved (today Hetti lives between Austria and Morocco); Bill Willis of course, who I mentioned before, as well as the Tazis; soon we met Mustapha Zine, a young notary, and his wife Houda, who were without a doubt the most good-looking couple in Morocco. I do not write these names with nostalgia, but rather with emotion, as they remind me of an earlier Morocco, and a time that it seemed would continue forever.

Jacqueline Foissac

Hetti von Bohlen

Mustapha and Houda Zine

Many friends came to visit us
at Dar el Hanch.

Fernando and Yves

Yves' longest friendship was with
Fernando Sanchez. The two young men
had met in Paris at the Chambre
Syndicale de la Couture, where they were
studying fashion. They had a strong
and enduring frienship. Fernando was
pursuing his career in New York, but would
see us often in Marrakech, as he ended up
buying our first home, Dar el Hanch.
He died of AIDS, several years before Yves
passed away.

Loulou de la Falaise and Fernando Sanchez

Loulou

Louise de La Falaise was the half-British daughter of Maxime de La Falaise, who played an important role in the world of fashion. Loulou seduced Yves with her eccentricity and audacity. She was his assistant for over 30 years; for a long time she was responsible for designing jewelry and hats.
We were introduced to Loulou by Fernando Sanchez. She married Thadée Klossowski, the son of the painter, Balthus. Both are friends who were very dear to us.

Jalil and Tamy Tazi were our first Moroccan friends. Tamy later opened a Saint Laurent Rive Gauche boutique in Casablanca. She's also a talented designer who takes inspiration from traditional culture without forgetting the times in which we live.

Tami Tazi and Yves
at a picnic given
by the Tazis

Joe McPhillips

When we met Joe McPhillips, he was the partner of the writer, John Hopkins. He would later become the headmaster of the American School in Tangier.

Yves designed the costumes for the annual play that Joe's students would perform. That year it was "The Bacchantes" by Euripides. The drawings are among the most beautiful ever done by Yves.

Andy Warhol came to visit us twice in Marrakech. He was accompanied by his friend Fred Hughes, who was his agent and dealer, as well as by his companion Jed Johnson. We liked them very much and had an unfailing admiration for Andy. It was always a pleasure to spend time with him. He was curious about everything, and would never cease asking questions and expressing a childlike amazement.

Andy Warhol

Yves and Bianca
Jagger

Loulou and Fernando

Yves, François-Marie Banier
and Hazel

The countess Charles de Breteuil was
without a doubt the Queen of Marrakech.
We called her Boul; she reigned over
the local expatriate community. She
would elegantly welcome guests at the
beautiful Villa Taylor, but disliked
those who were late. She and Yves were
very close. She fell on hard times and
opened her home to paying guests. But
not just anyone — you had to prove your
credentials. When she died, something
irreplaceable in Marrakech left with her.

Salon bleu - villa Taylor

In 1923, the architect Poisson
built the Villa Taylor, which later
became the home of Boul de Breteuil.
After the Casablanca Conference in
1943, Winston Churchill and F.D.
Roosevelt both stayed there.

Bill Willis' hard-to-find home was
located in the far recesses of the Sidi Bel-
Abbès neighborhood of the Medina. He
lived there until his death in 2009.

Dar Es Saada.

In 1975, Dar es Saada became our second home. We entrusted the renovation to Bill Willis; it would be one of his greatest achievements.

Sidi Mimoun, Paul and Talitha Getty's Palace
— which belongs today to Bernard-Henri Lévy —
where we spent so many magical evenings.

Bill Willis

He created the modern Moroccan
design movement. All the decorators
here were inspired by his work, and
his influence can be seen in homes,
palaces and hotels.

Quito Fierro as a child when I met him,
Adolfo de Velasco, and HRH Lalla Nafissa.

Yves and me at Dar es Saada

Yves at Dar es Saada

When he was younger, Yves liked
going to the souks and walking
in the famous Djemaa el Fna square.
The acrobats, snake charmers, and
gnaoua dancers fascinated him.

In the countryside

Yves at Dar el Hanch

Dar es Saada

Dar es Saada

Dar es Saada

Yves at Dar es Saada

Yves at the Jardin Majorelle

A drawing by Fernando Sanchez,
from left to right; Fernando,
Yves, Loulou, and me

A drawing by Yves
A study for a pergola

A drawing by Yves
A study for an entryway

A drawing by Yves. A study for a garden.

Yves was constantly drawing, just for pleasure. From his imagination would obviously spring dresses, but also gardens that would never be planted or realized.

Dar es Saada. Yves and me.

Dar es Saada.

YVES

Shortly after our arrival in Marrakech, we discovered the Jardin Majorelle. We didn't know much about Jacques Majorelle, except that he had been the son of Louis Majorelle, the famous furniture designer of the Ecole de Nancy. We learned that he had arrived in Morocco in 1917, invited by Marshal Lyautey, and that in 1922 he built a house which became known as the Villa Majorelle. At the time, it was located in the countryside. It was here that the Palmeraie (palm grove) began. Very quickly we became acquainted with the garden; there was rarely a day that went by when we didn't visit it. It was open to the public, but practically no one was ever there. We were enchanted by this oasis where Matisse colors blended with those of nature. When we purchased our second home, Dar es Saada, it was located in this special and privileged neighborhood that Marrakechis know well.

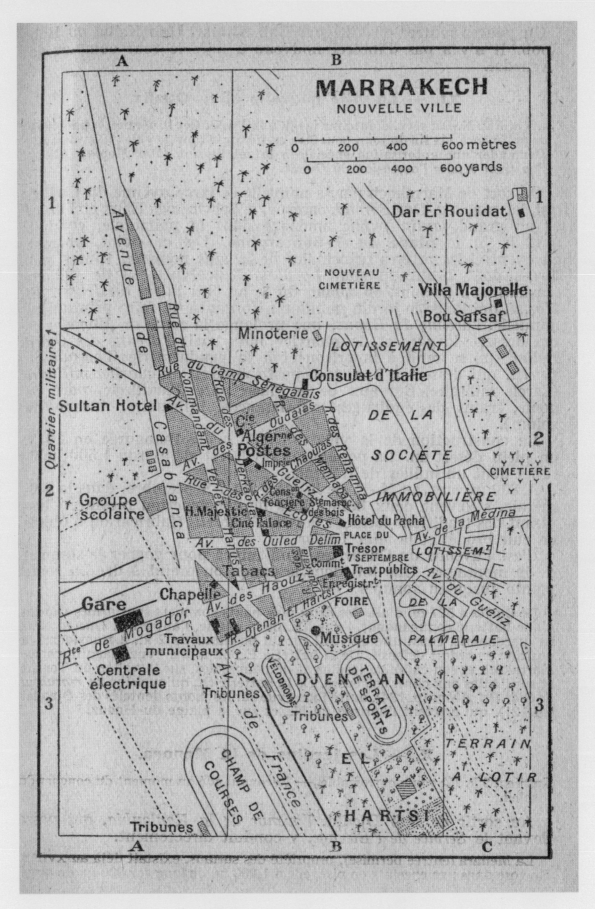

A map of the European neighborhoods of Marrakech in 1930. The Villa Majorelle can be seen towards the upper right among the palm trees.

When we learned that the nearby garden was going to be sold and replaced by a hotel, we did what seemed impossible at the time to stop the project. This is how one day we became the owners of the garden and its villa. Over the years, we brought the garden back to life. We decided to live in the villa, and named it the Villa Oasis, after the title of a book by Eugène Dabit. After Yves died, I donated everything to the foundation in Paris that bears both our names,

Yves at the Villa Oasis

Yves near Marrakech

Jacques Majorelle's villa is a painter's house, much in the same way that his garden is a painter's garden. He knew how to employ Moroccan art and craftsmanship, without falling into a decorative trap. He sparingly used Moroccan zelliges, zouacs and gebs, yet knew how to imbue his home with that perfume so unique to Marrakech. Nevertheless, when we purchased it in 1980, the house was in a sad state of conservation. Bill Willis, who we asked to oversee the restoration, worked wonders. He transformed it, yet kept Majorelle's essence and spirit. It goes without saying that this house owes everything to him. His talent and genius are deeply present everywhere in the villa. He created new spaces: a library built entirely with sculpted and painted wood, and a pavilion that overlooks an ornamental pond filled with water lilies.

Everywhere one turns, there is a trace of Bill that lives on today.

Yves in the blue living room at the
Villa Oasis

When Bill's work was done, Jacques Grange
chose the furniture and fabrics, in a
playful and joyous spirit that reflected
the house. Yves quickly felt at home here
and would visit often.

Mon cher Pierre

En ce jour de ton anniversaire, Je
me suis permis de prononcer quelques
mots qui viennent du plus profond de
Mon Coeur,

Les années passent, mais les
sentiments nobles et généreux
demeurent,

Sans Toi, Je ne serais peut être
pas celui que je suis.
Sans Moi je ne l'espère pas
mais je le pense, tu ne serais pas ce
que tu es.

Ce grand sigle à deux Têtes
qui cingle les mers, dépasse
les Frontières, envahit le monde
de son envergure sans pareil
pense c'est Nous. Et quand je dis Nous Je
pense. ~~c'est Toi~~. Avant Tout c'est Toi, Je te remercie d'être
Joyeux anniversaire Pierrot La
tendresse
                    Yves 14 Novembre 1987

A letter that Yves read on my birthday at
the Villa Oasis in Marrakech.
            (Translation page 90)

54

Yves at work

Yves would come to Marrakech every year on December 1 and June 1, to design his Haute Couture collections. He would work tirelessly for two weeks, and would return to Paris with an impressive dossier of drawings. It was in Marrakech that Yves discovered color. The rainbow of colors found in Morocco had a lifelong influence on him. He would awaken at an early hour, work for quite some time, and towards 5:00 in the afternoon we would go somewhere in the car. Either to the Ourika Valley, the Agnedal, or the countryside. We would take advantage of the moment and let the dogs run. We would often contemplate the sun, "drowning in its thickening blood".

When the runway models, one after the other, would later present Yves' collections, there was always a Moroccan scent in the air. It seemed to escape from the drawings he had done in the shade of palm trees,

Madison at Marrella Agnelli's home.

Madison Cox entered our lives in 1980 and never left. A renowned landscape architect, he is today the Director of the Jardin Majorelle and Vice President of the Pierre Bergé Yves Saint Laurent Foundation. It is thanks to him that the Jardin Majorelle and Villa Oasis are experiencing a renaissance. He is my closest friend, and I am counting on Madison to continue the work we've been doing.

I still remember when Marie-Hélène de Rothschild enthusiastically told me she was going to build a home in the Palmeraie. On our advice, she worked with Bill Willis, and the result was marvelous. Geoffrey Bennison added his "British touch" to the decoration. We spent many delightful moments there with her husband, Guy, and her inseparable friend, Alexis de Redé. The house was called "Dar Zuylen" after Marie-Hélène's maiden name. In Morocco, she was able to successfully replicate her world renowned "art de vivre." We were grief-stricken when she died.

Marie-Hélène de Rothschild
at Alexis de Redé's Oriental Ball

In 2000, Marella Agnelli decided to settle in
Marrakech. Yves and I were delighted, as we
loved and had admired her for many years. We
introduced Madison Cox to Marella; he created
one of the most beautiful gardens ever for her.

To join Marella for lunch at Ain Kassimou is
always a pleasure. Every time we are greeted
by her Japanese dog, and always find something
that surprises and amazes us — everything
is effortless and uncomplicated, yet so refined.
This is the very essence of Marella.

Yves and Catherine Deneuve at the Villa Oasis

Loulou and Thadée Klossowski

60

José and
Ann-Marie
Muñoz

Moujik

Loulou, Fernando, Yves, and Thadée

Yves and me at Dar el Hanch

A serpent painted by Yves in the dining room at Dar el Hanch

Yves, Jacques Grange, me, and Fernando

François and Betty Catroux, and Yves

Yves and Marian McEvoy
a journalist at Woman's Wear Daily
and longtime friend

Yves at Dar el Hanch

Yves met Anne-Marie Muñoz the day he arrived at Christian Dior; she was already working there. They very quickly became inseparable friends. She worked alongside Yves for 40 years as Director of his studio, and played a major role at the house of YSL. She was a master at combining authority and an attention to detail, always with a tender heart that was natural to her. Yves loved and respected her. She and her husband, José, were loyal friends.

Yves and Anne-Marie
in the studio of the fashion house

Yves and Betty

Yves met Betty before she married the decorator François Catroux. He immediately knew she was the ideal woman to wear his clothes. She was one of the first to daringly wear a pantsuit, "Le Smoking", or a jumpsuit. She and François have always been our perfect friends. We hope to have returned this deep friendship in kind.

An Yves Saint Laurent drawing.

Our first house was called Dar el Hanch. In Arabic, "hanch" means snake. Is this perhaps why Yves always drew so many? Snakes are found nearly everywhere in his work.

Morocco-inspired drawings by Yves for an
Haute couture collection.

Yves

Bill and Yves

Yves

Me

Yves

With Yves, listening to frogs hidden among the papyrus.

Jacques Majorelle's studio that we transformed
into a museum.

Yves and me at the Jardin Majorelle.

I'm very fond of this photo as it's the only one
that exists of the two of us at the Jardin Majorelle.
It was taken by Didier Feivre in the early 1980s.
We dearly loved Didier, who was later to die
of AIDS. He was intelligent and enthusiastic. He
was Yves' doctor, and took very good care of him.
I miss him, as I miss all of those who have been
killed by this illness: Patrick, Kim, Joël, Giuseppe,
Jorge, Fernando, José, and so many others,

All his life and only while at home, Yves loved wearing Moroccan cotton clothes made by Boujemaa, an artisan who also raised parrots.

Tangier, where the shades of Paul Bowles, Kerouac, Burroughs, Morand, Brion Gysin, Ira Belline, Barbara Hutton, Matisse, Genet, and so many others brush against each other; Tangier, where thanks to Bowles, the Rolling Stones discovered Jajouka music; Tangier, a city that's not entirely Moroccan and that seems in conversation with Europe, a city where so many languages are spoken; Tangier and its Librairie des Colonnes, where so many writers were welcomed, including André Gide. Beginning in 1999, Tangier is where Yves chose to spend the summer months at the Villa Mabrouka, our home clinging to the cliffs just a stone's throw from the casbah.

Yves and me in Tangier
at the Villa Mabrouka.

We came often to Tangier and its endless beaches.
At the time, we would rent a car and discover
the countryside. An evening tea in the Petit
Socco became nearly a ritual for us. The Villa
Mabrouka, and its garden and pool, were
large and beautiful. Unfortunately, Yves,
was often sick here, so our stays in Tangier
were less joyful than we desired.
Nevertheless, we loved this city – I still
love it, more and more – and we never
regretted our decision to come here.

Yves and Moujik in Tangier, in
the pool of the Villa Mabrouka.

Villa Mabrouka.

Tangier : Cape Spartel

We were friends in Tangier with the antique dealer, Boukker Temli, and his wife, Nour. It is thanks to them that we were able to organize an exhibit of Moroccan caftans at our foundation in Paris.

At Boukker's home we would often see the writer Tahar ben Jelloun, as well as our dear and longtime friend Christopher Gibbs.

When Alberto Pinto lived in Tangier, he owned a "1001 Nights" palace, which he decorated in his unique style.

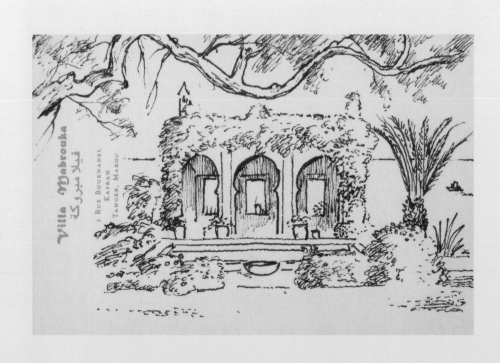

Boubker Temli, Jacqueline Foissac, Nom Temli,
Didier Fèvre, and Jacques Grange.

When we were younger, we would spend long days on the beaches that extend beyond the Diplomatic Forest.

The dancer Jorge Lago in Tangier.

Jorge was a member of the Cuban National
Ballet, under the direction of the great Alicia
Alonzo. He declared asylum in France after
a series of performances in Paris. He became the
partner of Zizi Jeanmaire at the Casino de Paris.
It was there that Yves and I met him.

Yves would often enjoy an afternoon mint tea at the Café Hafa. Situated atop a cliff and built around several terraces, it is popular with young, sea-gazing Moroccans. The cats seem to run the show at this café, which is undoubtedly one of the most picturesque places in Tangier.

Tangier, facing the sea, the Café Hafa.

Yves died at his Paris residence on June 1, 2008
of a brain cancer. More than a year earlier, the
doctors had warned me there was no remedy or
hope, that it was fatal. After several days
in a coma, he passed away peacefully.
Several months before Yves died, I asked Madison
Cox to build a memorial for Yves in the Jardin
Majorelle. He brought a Roman column from
our home in Tangier that had been found on the
beach. He placed it between two white marble benches,
buried it beneath lush strelitzia, and added a
plaque that bears Yves' name. Here one can gather
one's thoughts and think of him.
His ashes were scattered among the roses at the
Villa Oasis. More than six hundred thousand
people visit the garden every year. Many among
them stop for a while at the memorial, or
photograph it. It pleases me that they think
of Yves, that they remember him and his work.
Artists have a way of not really dying.

Memorial

Glossary

bab: gate

dar: House

derb: small street

gebs: sculpted plaster

Zelliges: ceramic tiles

Zouacs: painted wood

Acknowledgments.

Graphic design: Alexandre Wolkoff
assisted by Camille Vinkinderen
Wolkoff and Arnodin Agency

Fondation Pierre Bergé - Yves Saint Laurent:
Dominique Deroche, Kamel Khemissi,
Connie Uzzo and, Pauline Vidal.

Translation by José Abete

on the facing page
An advertisement shot at the Menara gardens,
Marrakech.
Photograph by Sacha.
MAFIA Agency

Translation of the speech made by Yves on my birthday (page 54).

My dear Pierre,
Today, on your birthday, I would like to say a few words that come from the bottom of my heart.
Years go by, but deep and noble feelings remain.
Without you, I might not be who I am.
Without me — I don't hope so, but it's what I think — you wouldn't be who you are.
This great two-headed eagle lashes the seas, soaring beyond borders, and fills the world with its incomparable wingspan.
That is who we are. And when I say we, I think above all it's you.
Thank you for being there.
Happy anniversary, Pierrot la tendresse.

Yves   14 November 1987

PHOTOGRAPHIC CREDITS

Page 9 : © Pierre Bergé

Page 11 (top and bottom) : © Pierre Bergé

Page 13 : © Reginald Gray

Page 18 : Patrick Lichfield / *Vogue USA* / Condé Nast Archive. © Condé Nast

Page 19 : © Pierre Bergé

Page 20 : Patrick Lichfield / *Vogue USA* / Condé Nast Archive. © Condé Nast

Page 21 (top) : © Pierre Bergé

Page 21 (bottom) : © Yves Saint Laurent

Page 29 (bottom) : © Pierre Bergé

Page 31 (top) : © Pierre Bergé

Page 36 (top) : © Pierre Bergé

Page 37 (top and bottom) : © Fondation Pierre Bergé – Yves Saint Laurent / Guy Marineau

Pages 38 et 39 (top and bottom) : Reginald Gray / *W Magazine* / Condé Nast Archive. © Condé Nast

Page 40 (top and bottom) : © Pierre Bergé

Page 41 (top) : © François-Marie Banier

Page 41 (bottom left and right) : © Pierre Bergé

Page 42 (top) : © Fondation Pierre Bergé – Yves Saint Laurent / Guy Marineau

Page 42 (bottom) : © Pierre Bergé

Page 46 (top) : © François-Marie Banier

Page 47 (top right and bottom left) : © Pierre Boulat courtesy Association Pierre et Alexandra Boulat

Page 47 (top left and bottom right) : © Pierre Bergé

Page 49 : *Guide bleu Maroc* 1930. Fonds Hachette / IMEC

Page 51 (top and bottom) : © Pierre Bergé

Page 53 : © André Rau

Page 55 : © Pierre Boulat courtesy Association Pierre et Alexandra Boulat

Page 57 : © Doris Brynner

Page 58 : André Ostier © Beneficiaries of photographer

Page 59 : © Doris Brynner

Page 60 (top) : © André Rau

Page 62 (bottom) : © François-Marie Banier

Page 63 (middle) : © Fondation Pierre Bergé – Yves Saint Laurent / Guy Marineau

Page 64 : © Pierre Boulat courtesy Association Pierre et Alexandra Boulat

Page 68 (the four large photos) : © Pierre Bergé

Page 69 : © Pierre Boulat courtesy Association Pierre et Alexandra Boulat

Page 71 : © Didier Fèvre

Page 72 (top) : © Fondation Pierre Bergé – Yves Saint Laurent / Guy Marineau

Page 77 : © Philippe Mugnier

Page 83 : © Pierre Bergé

Page 87 : © Pierre Thoretton

Page 89 : © Sacha / Mafia

Translation : José Abete

Cataloging-in-Publication Data has been applied for and may be obtained from the Library of Congress.

ISBN: 978-1-4197-1349-1

Printed and bound in Italy
10 9 8 7 6 5 4 3 2 1

Abrams books are available at special discounts when purchased in quantity for premiums and promotions as well as fundraising or educational use. Special editions can also be created to specification. For details, contact specialsales@abramsbooks.com or the address below.

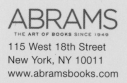

115 West 18th Street
New York, NY 10011
www.abramsbooks.com